Native AMERICANS

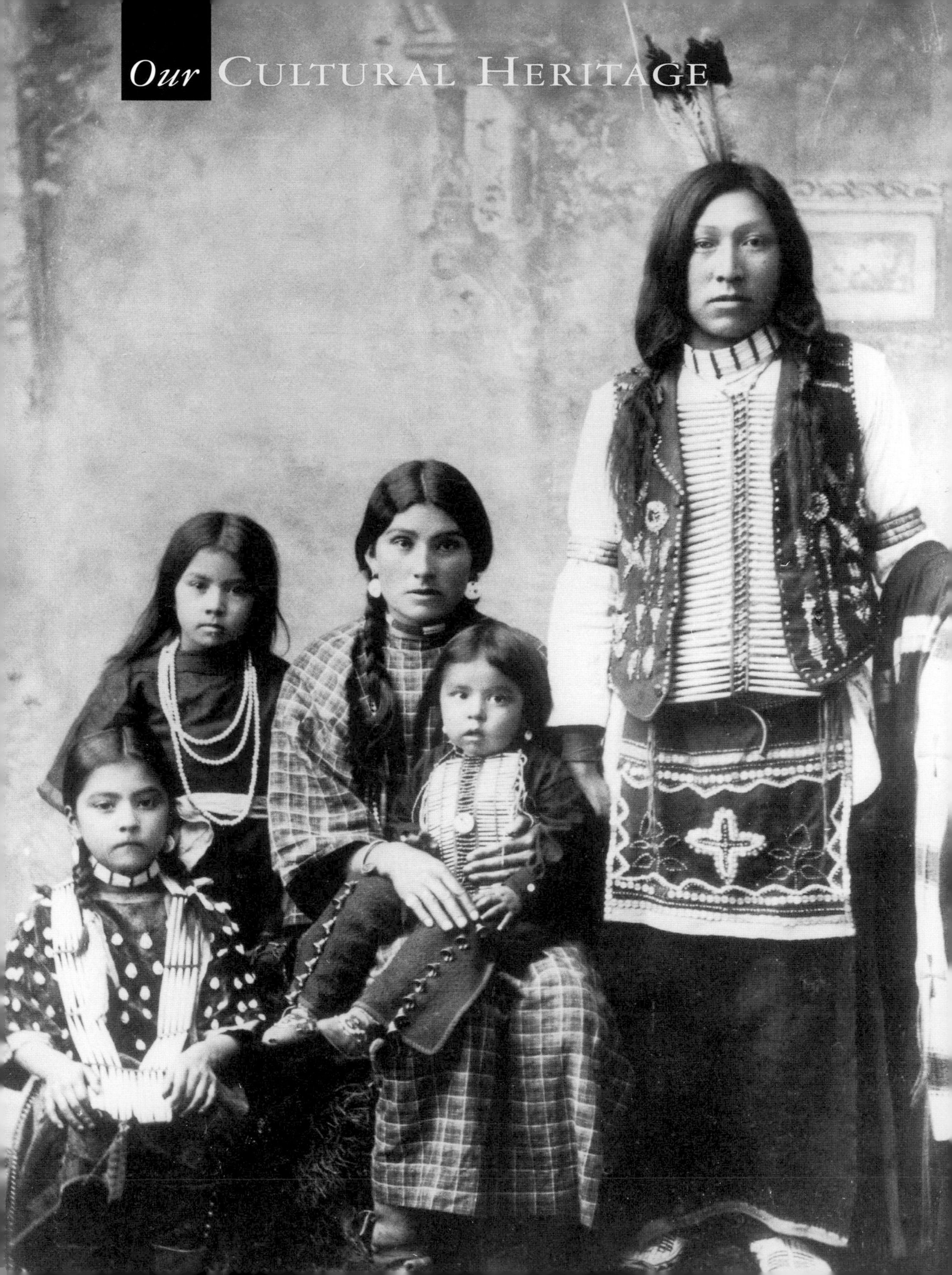
Our Cultural Heritage

SPIRIT
of America®

Native AMERICANS

By Judy Alter

The Child's World®
Chanhassen, Minnesota

6

Native AMERICANS

Published in the United States of America by The Child's World®
PO Box 326 • Chanhassen, MN 55317-0326 • 800-599-READ • www.childsworld.com

Acknowledgments
The Child's World®: Mary Berendes, Publishing Director

Editorial Directions, Inc.: E. Russell Primm, Emily Dolbear, Sarah E. De Capua, and Lucia Raatma, Editors; Linda S. Koutris, Photo Selector; Image Select International, Photo Research; Red Line Editorial and Pam Rosenberg, Fact Research; Tim Griffin/IndexServ, Indexer; Chad Rubel, Proofreader

Photos
Cover/frontispiece: A Native American family on an Idaho reservation in 1897

Cover photographs ©: AKG Images, Berlin; Suzanne Murphy/FPG International

Interior photographs ©: AKG-Images, Berlin, 6; Corbis, 7, 8; Getty Images, 10,11,12, 13; Western History/Genealogy Department, Denver Public Library, 14, 15; Corbis, 16, 18, 19; Western History/Genealogy Department, Denver Public Library, 20; TRIP/E. Smith, 21; TRIP/J. Greenberg, 22; Corbis, 23; TRIP/D. Cole, 24; Getty Images, 25 top; TRIP/M. Barlow, 25 bottom; Getty Images, 26; Western History/Genealogy Department, Denver Public Library, 27; TRIP/ M. Barlow, 28.

Library of Congress Cataloging-in-Publication Data
Alter, Judy, 1938–
 Native Americans / by Judy Alter.
   p. cm.
Includes bibliographical references and index.
Summary: Introduces the major customs, heritage, and history of Native Americans, including a glimpse of how these have influenced Anglo-American culture.
 ISBN 1-56766-152-1 (lib. bdg. : alk. paper)
 1. Indians of North America—Social life and customs—Juvenile literature. [1. Indians of North America.] I. Title.
 E98.S7 A58 2002
 973.04'97—dc21
                    2001007807

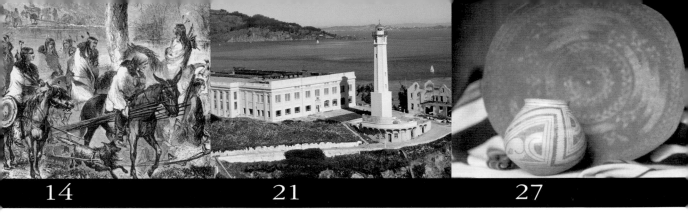

14   21   27

Contents

Chapter ONE

A Clash of Cultures

Christopher Columbus reaching the American continent in October 1492

WHEN ITALIAN EXPLORER CHRISTOPHER Columbus "discovered" America in 1492, Native Americans had been living here for about 12,000 years. As many as 40 million Native Americans were living on the North American continent. These ancient people probably crossed the Bering land bridge, a strip of land that connected Russia to Alaska at that time. The land bridge is now underwater, covered by the Bering Strait.

Over several thousand years, most of these people drifted south into what is now the United States. Some went even farther—to Central and South America. Others went north and east to Canada.

The Tlingit and other northwestern Pacific Indians were the richest of the **pre-Columbian Indians**. They had plenty of fish and other food. They lived in permanent villages. The Midwest was home to subtribes of the Iroquois. The Mohawk, Oneida, Onondaga, Cayuga, and Seneca people were farmers who also lived in villages. They grew corn, beans, and squash.

With the introduction of horses, Native Americans followed and hunted the buffalo herds.

In the northern woodlands (now New England), the Algonquin people were also **nomadic** hunters and trappers. They moved from place to place looking for food. The Plains Indians—Blackfeet, Piegan, Gros Ventres, and Cree—were also wanderers. In the 1500s, Spanish explorers brought them horses. As they followed the buffalo herds, the Plains Indians became even more

A Native American village

nomadic. They also became warlike. They raided camps and stole horses, to win **coup** for bravery, and to gain or protect territory. In later years, the Comanche and Kiowa would rule the Plains.

In the Southwest, the Anasazi people had developed a sophisticated civilization by A.D. 900. They grew corn, squash, and beans. They lived in multilevel dwellings carved into cliffs below the **mesas**. These dwellings can still be seen at Canyon de Chelly (duh-SHAY) near Chinle, Arizona. The Hopi, Zuni, and Pueblo peoples later occupied such dwellings. In the 1700s, the warlike Navajo took them over.

Highly civilized tribes such as the Cahokia and Tamaroa lived in today's Midwest and the southern woodlands. They hunted, gathered fruits and berries, traded with other tribes, farmed, and occasionally took slaves from other tribes. The Cahokia built ceremonial burial mounds that date to the early 1300s. Today, the Cahokia do not exist. Some of the largest mounds, however, are preserved in a state park in Cahokia, Illinois.

Neither today's American Indians nor the landscape are like they were then. Dense forests existed where cities and fields now stand. Even the courses of the rivers have changed. Many animals have disappeared.

Christopher Columbus never saw mainland North America. He landed on the Caribbean island of Hispaniola, which today is made up of the countries of Haiti and the Dominican Republic. Spanish explorers and **conquistadors** were the first white people the Native Americans encountered. Hernando de Soto was the first conquistador to explore the eastern United States. Landing in Florida in 1539, he and his men traveled as far north as Lake Michigan. Then they turned south through Illinois, Missouri, Arkansas, and finally arrived in Texas. They stole from Indian villages wherever they went. They killed the men and took women, food, and slaves. In addition, they unknowingly infected the Indians with European diseases, such as **smallpox**.

In the Southwest, Francisco Vásquez de Coronado established the same pattern. He came from Mexico seeking gold. Coronado visited friendly Zuni pueblos, or villages, and made slaves of the Indians. Coronado's men killed many Zuni people. Coronado did not succeed at finding gold. Instead, he found only **turquoise**.

Hernando de Soto, the first conquistador to explore the eastern United States

Later explorers and settlers treated Native Americans no better. As soon as white settlers arrived in North America, Indians began giving up their land. In the early 1600s, Europeans began to immigrate in great numbers. This would continue for more than 300 years. As more settlers arrived and established large farms, less land was available for the Indians to live on. Other problems occurred when settlers killed many of the animals   the Native Americans relied on for food. As their problems worsened, the Indians waged war against the white settlers.

Francisco Vásquez de Coronado crossing the plains with a Native American guide

The first major Indian uprising was in 1638 in Virginia. The Pequot Indians and the Massachusetts Bay Colony went to war over settlement of the Connecticut River area. The Indians had rebelled against the settlers from time to time, killing a large number of whites, including women and children. The government of the colony finally attacked the Indians. Indian forts were burned, and men, women, and children were killed.

Indians lost land in **treaties** as well as in battle. U.S. authorities signed treaties with the leader of a tribe or with a small group of Indians. The U.S. authorities did not realize that an Indian leader did not always speak for the whole tribe. The Algonquin Indians were defeated by U.S. troops at the Battle of Fallen Timbers. Later, they lost much of the Ohio River Valley after signing the Treaty of Greenville.

English settlers and Native Americans fighting in the Pequot War

The Seminole people of Florida were persuaded to sign treaties giving up their land in exchange for food and supplies. However, they never received the food and supplies. After fighting two wars in their efforts to hold on to their land, the Seminoles were sent to the Oklahoma Territory.

THE CHEROKEE HAD SETTLED IN WESTERN GEORGIA AND ADOPTED EUROPEAN customs. They were farmers and cattle ranchers. They had roads, churches, and a central government. The people dressed like whites and some had even married white people. But the growing white population in Georgia wanted the Cherokee land.

A congressional act of 1830 gave the government the right to force Indians to move away from their lands. Cherokee leader John Ross (below) fought this in court. The U.S. Supreme Court ruled that the Cherokee were a sovereign nation and could not be removed.

In 1835, most Cherokee accepted John Ross as their leader. But a few followed Major Ridge. Major Ridge signed the Treaty of New Echota, agreeing to removal. This gave President Andrew Jackson the legal authority to remove all the Cherokee.

In 1838, General Winfield Scott's troops attacked the Cherokee Nation. Men, women, and children were taken from their homes and forced to march 1,000 miles (1,600 kilometers) to Oklahoma. The U.S. Army troops escorting the Native Americans rarely allowed them to stop for food, water, or rest. About 4,000 Cherokee died on the journey. The route they traveled became known as the Trail of Tears.

Chapter Two

More Battles

Native Americans being forced from their villages and taken to reservations

BY THE EARLY 1800s, THE U.S. GOVERNMENT had decided that the land west of the Mississippi River was of no use to white people. It was believed to be an ideal place to move Indians from the East, however. The government began sending the Indians to live on **reservations**. Most eastern tribes had been sent to reservations by 1861 when the Civil War began.

After the American Civil War (1861–1865), the U.S. Army sent its soldiers to conquer the Plains Indians.

Sioux Indians in a council circle at the Pine Ridge Reservation in South Dakota

These men were experienced soldiers, but they were not used to fighting Indians. The Plains Indians attacked **stagecoaches** and destroyed communication lines. There were many battles. The Indians attacked settlers moving west, and often killed them. Sometimes the Indians attacked first; other times, the soldiers attacked first.

The 1890 Battle of Wounded Knee in South Dakota ended the Indian Wars. By

A Native American
Ghost Dance

then the Sioux were confined to reservations, and the buffalo were almost extinct. A **shaman** named Wovoka started the Ghost Dance movement about that time. He predicted that the Ghost Dance would restore the prairie and the buffalo, destroy the whites, and bring dead Indians to life. Believers wore brightly colored Ghost Shirts that they thought would protect them from army bullets.

The Ghost Dance frightened whites at the reservations, and they called for help. An arrest order went out for many Indians, including Chief Big Foot of the Sioux. He decided to take his people to the Pine Ridge Reservation in South Dakota for safety. They camped on the edge of Wounded Knee Creek, surrounded by U.S. Army troops. On the morning of December 29, accidental gunfire suddenly erupted. After the smoke cleared, more than 150 Sioux were dead, including Big Foot.

In the late 19th century, government authorities decided that the best way to help the Indians was to teach them American ways and traditions. The authorities wanted the Indians to give up their way of life. Schools were established far from the reservations,

Young Sioux boys outside a dormitory at the Carlisle Indian School

and Indian children were forced to attend these schools. The most notorious was at Carlisle, Pennsylvania. There, Indian children were forced to dress like white children, but they were not taught academic subjects such as reading, writing, and arithmetic. They were taught **trades**. After graduating from Carlisle, they returned to their homes angry at the whites for attempting to rob them of their heritages.

By 1900, the number of Native Americans in the United States had shrunk to 250,000. About 1,000 of them lived in cities. The rest were on reservations.

THE BATTLE OF PALO DURO CANYON IS ONE OF THE LEAST-TOLD STORIES OF the Plains Indians Wars. In 1874, several Native American groups were camped on the floor of the large Palo Duro Canyon in northwestern Texas. On September 28, army troops under the command of Colonel Ranald Mackenzie (below) attacked at sunrise. The various Indian camps were too scattered in the canyon to make a unified defense.

The camps and supplies of the Native Americans were destroyed. Only three warriors and one white soldier died in the battle, but the Indians lost their winter food supply. Also, more than 1,400 of their ponies were captured. About 350 ponies were given to soldiers, and the remaining ponies were shot and killed. Without their food supplies or ponies on which to hunt the buffalo, the Indians could not survive. Knowing they had been defeated, they reluctantly went to the reservation.

The Battle of Palo Duro Canyon ended the freedom of the southern Plains Indians. It was their last attempt to resist the whites who were moving onto their land. The tribes forced to go to reservations after the battle included the Comanche, Kiowa, Kiowa Apache, Cheyenne, and Arapaho. When they reached the reservation, they were forbidden to leave to hunt buffalo. They had to learn to farm.

19

Chapter THREE

Problems to Solve

In the summer of 1968, about 200 Native Americans from all tribes met to discuss issues that concerned them all. They discussed poor housing, unemployment, lack of education, and federal policies affecting Native Americans. This meeting gave birth to the American Indian Movement (AIM).

Members of the American Indian Movement in a Denver, Colorado, office

Indians began to fight for their rights as U.S. citizens. They followed the pattern set by Martin Luther King Jr., who had fought peacefully for the rights of black Americans.

In November 1969, Indians from several tribes occupied Alcatraz Island off the California coast. The island had once been home to American Indians. More recently it had been a federal prison. Those who seized it wanted to make it a Native American cultural center and university. The Native Americans stayed for 19 months. When water and food supplies were no longer available, they had to leave. But they had brought the demands of Native Americans to the public's attention.

Native Americans seized and occupied Alcatraz Island for 19 months.

In the 1970s, people living on Indian reservations continued to face serious economic and social problems. Most people lived in poverty and many were alcoholics. Juvenile delinquency and all types of crime were high. Schools on reservations did not have adequate textbooks or supplies. American Indians experienced the lowest level of educational success

Interesting Fact

▶ During World War II (1939–1945), approximately 25,000 Native Americans served in the military and more than 50,000 worked in war industries.

Children at the Pottawatomi Reservation in Kansas

of any ethnic minority in the country. Faced with these problems, Indians pressed for the right to manage their own affairs. In 1975, the U.S. Congress passed the Indian Self-Determination and Education Assistance Act, which granted them this right.

Today, there are almost 2 million Native Americans in the United States. About one-third of them still live on reservations. Most of the reservations lie west of the Mississippi River and most are owned and governed by the Indians. The quality of life is still poor on most reservations. The Indians who live there have the highest unemployment rate in the United States, the lowest incomes, and the poorest health.

In spite of these challenges, many tribes have sought to solve their own problems by following the ancient ways of their ancestors. In the process, they have made many and varied contributions to the U.S. culture.

THE U.S. CONGRESS PASSED THE INDIAN GAMING Regulatory Act in 1988. According to that law, Indian reservations could open gambling **casinos** on their land if they were located in a state where gambling was legal. Of the 557 tribes in the United States, 90 of them operate 200 casinos in 19 states.

Unemployment and welfare rates have dropped significantly on reservations with casinos. Income from the casinos has been used to build schools, colleges, and community centers. Alcohol and drug treatment programs have been created. Water and sewer systems have been installed. Gambling casinos have improved life dramatically on some reservations, but older tribal members object to the casinos. They fear losing traditional Native American values.

23

Chapter FOUR

Powwows and Potters

Native American jewelry and other crafts have become an important part of American culture.

PERHAPS THE BIGGEST CONTRIBUTION NATIVE Americans have made to American culture is in the language. Countless cities, rivers, and states bear Indian names, including Chicago, Connecticut, Illinois, Massachusetts, and Miami. Counties throughout the country are named after tribes, such as Cherokee, Cheyenne, and Algonquin.

Indian contributions to American culture are most obvious in the American Southwest. There, many men and women wear turquoise jewelry, such as belt buckles and the elaborate squash-blossom necklaces made of silver and often studded with turquoise. Long skirts that swirl about the ankles are popular among women in the Southwest.

Native American music
and celebrations have not
become a part of popular
American entertainment. But
many American Indians
today belong to local tribal
societies. They meet at least
once a year to perform traditional dances in
traditional costumes and sing the songs of
their ancestors. These celebrations, often
called powwows, have become
popular with American
tourists, especially in the
Southwest.

*Sioux dancers at a
powwow on a South
Dakota reservation*

*A Navajo weaver creating
a beautiful rug*

Native American art and
literature have been more
successful in mainstream
America. People in many parts
of the country collect silver
and turquoise jewelry. Navajo
rugs are in demand throughout the United States and an
older rug of good quality can
sell for thousands of dollars.

Maria Montoya Martínez,
known simply as Maria, is the

Interesting Fact

▸ The Native American Rights Fund was established in 1970 to furnish legal aid to protect Indian lands and resources.

best-known potter in the Southwest today. Maria lived in a small New Mexico pueblo known as San Ildefonso and spoke Tewa—her native language—and Spanish. She made ancient black pottery—pottery blackened by exposure to smoke in a special firing process. Today, a black pot by Maria is very valuable. Maria died in 1980, but she taught many other pueblo women her techniques. Their work is also valuable today.

In the 1970s, artist R. C. Gorman of Santa Fe, New Mexico, created stylized pictures of Native American women. These were turned into posters, prints, and greeting cards. Gorman's work was extremely popular in Santa Fe for many years.

Kiowa and Cherokee author and poet N. Scott Momaday, a professor of English at the University of Arizona, has written several novels. *House Made of Dawn* won the 1969 **Pulitzer Prize** for literature. In *Rainy Mountain*, another

Pulitzer Prize–winning writer Scott Momaday

well-known work of Momaday's, he carefully preserves the storytelling tradition of his tribal ancestors.

Louise Erdrich is a poet, short-story writer, and novelist. A Chippewa born in Minnesota, she was raised in North Dakota by parents who worked for the Bureau of Indian Affairs. Her work deals with the identity problems faced by Indians in a white society. Her many books include *The Beet Queen*, *The Antelope Wife*, and *Love Medicine*.

Native American pottery is known for its intricate patterns.

Native American culture has entered American life in both authentic and popular, or commercial, forms. Years ago, wooden Indians were the symbol of tobacco shops. Today, professional sports teams such as baseball's Atlanta Braves and football's Washington Redskins, along with college and high-school sports teams named the Chieftains and the Mohawks honor the history of Native Americans in the United States.

Interesting Fact

▶ From 1961 to 1971, Benjamin Reifel, a Sioux Indian, served as a U.S. congressman from South Dakota.

Interesting Fact

Chief Joseph of the Nez Percé gave the most famous Indian speech of surrender. In North America, U.S. soldiers had chased his people to within 40 miles (64 kilometers) of safety in Canada. But the Indians were too tired, hungry, and cold to go any farther. Chief Joseph told the soldiers, "From where the sun now stands, I will fight no more forever."

The true importance of the Native American heritage to American culture is seen in the cliff dwellings at Canyon de Chelly, the burial mounds in Illinois, and countless other authentic Native American sites. Many are preserved as state parks throughout the nation. They offer Americans of all ethnic backgrounds a chance to experience and understand the importance of the nation's Native American heritage.

Today, visitors can see Navajo dwellings at Canyon de Chelly in Arizona.

11,000 B.C. Asian people cross the Bering land bridge to what is now North America.

1492 Christopher Columbus sails to the Americas.

1540 Hernando de Soto lands in Florida. Francisco Vásquez de Coronado explores the Southwest in search of gold.

1637–1638 The Pequot War erupts.

1770s Some Indians fight for the British during the Revolutionary War.

1812 Indians fight for the British in the War of 1812.

1800s The U.S. government begins to remove Native Americans from their lands to reservations west of the Mississippi River.

1832 Black Hawk's War ends with removal of the Sauk and Fox peoples to Indian (Oklahoma) Territory.

1838 Seminoles are forced to leave Florida.

1864 Chief Black Kettle's band of Cheyenne die in a brutal massacre.

1876 The Battle of the Little Big Horn takes place in Montana.

1877 Chief Joseph surrenders the Nez Percé to the U.S. Army with a moving speech.

1884 Most Apaches are confined to reservations. Apache chief Geronimo is still rebellious.

1890 The Battle of Wounded Knee ends the Indian Wars.

1968 Indian leaders form the American Indian Movement.

1969 A group of Native Americans seize Alcatraz Island and occupy it for 19 months.

1988 The Indian Gaming Regulatory Act is passed.

Bureau of Indian Affairs (BIA)
The BIA is an agency of the U.S. government that promotes the welfare of Native Americans.

casinos (kuh-SEE-nohz)
Casinos are buildings used for gambling. Many American Indian tribes have established casinos in certain states.

conquistadors (kon-KEES-tuh-dorz)
Conquistadors were Spanish explorers who conquered America in the 16th century. These explorers fought with Native Americans and spread deadly diseases among their tribes.

coup (KOO)
A coup is a highly successful move or action. For Native Americans, it was an act of exceptional bravery in battle.

mesas (MAY-suz)
Mesas are hills with steep sides and flat tops. Native Americans lived in dwellings carved into cliffs below mesas.

nomadic (noh-MAD-ik)
People who travel from place to place seeking food are nomadic. The Algonquin Indians were nomadic.

pre-Columbian Indians (pree-kuh-LUHM-bee-uhn IN-dee-uhnz)
Native Americans who lived in North American before Columbus's voyage to America in 1492 were pre-Columbian Indians.

Pulitzer Prize (puh-LIT-sur PRIZE)
Pulitzer Prizes are given each year to award excellence in writing. Scott Momaday won the Pulitzer Prize for literature in 1969.

reservations (rez-ur-VAY-shuhnz)
Reservations are areas set aside for Native Americans. When white settlers took control of their land, Native Americans were forced onto reservations.

shaman (SHAH-muhn)
A shaman is a medicine man who uses magic to cure the sick and control events. Wovoka was an Indian shaman.

smallpox (SMAWL-poks)
Smallpox is a contagious disease known for causing high fevers and open sores. Native Americans sometimes caught smallpox from infected blankets traded by explorers.

stagecoaches (STAYJ-koh-chez)
Stagecoaches were coaches pulled by horses and used to carry passengers and mail between designated locations. Some Native Americans attacked stagecoaches as a way to fight white settlers.

trades (TRAYDZ)
Trades are jobs or crafts that require working with the hands or with machines. On some reservation schools, Native Americans were taught only trades rather than academic subjects.

treaties (TREE-teez)
Treaties are agreements between groups of people. American Indians lost some of their land through treaties signed with the U.S. government.

turquoise (TUR-kwoyz)
A turquoise is a blue-green stone mined in the Southwest. Native Americans are known for creating beautiful turquoise jewelry.

Internet Sites

Visit our homepage for lots of links about Native Americans:
http://www.childsworld.com/links.html

Note to Parents, Teachers, and Librarians:
We routinely verify our Web links to make sure they're safe,
active sites—so encourage your readers to check them out!

Books

Barth, Kelly L. *Native Americans of the Northwest Plateau.* Minneapolis: Lucent, 2001.

Buller, Laura. *Secret Worlds: Native Americans.* New York: DK Publishing, 2001.

Ciment, James, Ph.D., with Ronald LaFrance, Ph.D. *Scholastic Encyclopedia of the Native American Indian.* New York: Scholastic, 1996.

Clare, John D. *American Indian Life.* New York: Barron's Juveniles, 2000.

Yue, Charlotte and David. *The Wigwam and the Longhouse.* New York: Houghton Mifflin, 2000.

Places to Visit or Contact

Museum of the Cherokee Indian
Route 441 and Drama Road
P.O. Box 1599
Cherokee, NC 28719
828-497-3481

Museum of Indian Arts and Culture
710 Camino Lejo
Santa Fe, NM 87504
505-476-1250

National Museum of the American Indian
Cultural Resources Center
4220 Silver Hill Road
Suitland, MD 20746
201-238-6624

Index